Did I Marry Him?
An ordinary day with a
Fairly Normal Christian Wife
By Michelle Stimpson

Edited by: Michelle Chester, ebm-services.com
Cover Design by: Ranilo Cablo

Copyright © 2011 Michelle Stimpson
All rights reserved.
ISBN: 1461186528
ISBN-13: 978-1461186526

Fiction by Michelle Stimpson

Boaz Brown
Divas of Damascus Road
Trouble in My Way
The Good Stuff
Last Temptation
Someone to Watch Over Me

Table of Contents

	Introduction	5
1	We Started Off Wrong	9
2	I Think I Married the Wrong Guy	13
3	I'm Just Not That Into Sex	17
4	We've Grown Apart	23
5	I Miss the Thrill of Being Single	27
6	I Love My Husband, but I'm Not In Love	31
7	We've Got Parenting Issues	35
8	I Feel Trapped	39
9	This Submission Thing is Ridiculous	43
10	He's Not Who I Thought He Was	47
11	I Can't Tolerate This Snoring Anymore!	51
12	I Don't Think I Can Do This Domestic Stuff	57
13	Watching My Parents Messed Me Up	61
14	Sometimes, He's Just Lazy	65
15	What Am I Supposed to Do Now?	69
	Recommended Readings	77

Introduction

You never really know exactly what you're signing up for when you get married. Granted, you can do your best to prepare by reading books, spending time with your future husband, and praying about the relationship. But you can't know until you know.

The purpose of this semi-memoir is to share the few things I *think* I know after seventeen years of marriage, and to strengthen other wives who may be wondering what on earth they've gotten themselves into with this whole marriage thing. Don't get me wrong: I love my husband and I'm acutely aware that marriage symbolizes Christ's covenant with the church. But I have pondered every question addressed in this book at one point or another. I thought the fact that I wondered these things meant maybe I was headed for divorce court. Or maybe I wasn't really much of a Christian because, after all, what kind of Christian wife misses the thrill of her single days (see chapter five)?

I wished I'd known and trusted someone well enough to discuss these issues with them, but I figured some people were already betting Stevie and I would be divorced by the time we hit twenty-five (for good reason), so I kept my mouth shut, watched Lifetime movies and Divorce Court to try and figure out what *not* to do about my feelings. And I prayed. God worked a miracle in our marriage. He tore the whole thing down and rebuilt it from the ground up.

He helped me through past issues and the ones I have even now when my husband and I fuss about which of us probably misplaced the remote control. Again.

To understand this book and fully grasp the extent of God's intervention, you have to know that Stevie and I started off all wrong (see Chapter 1). Despite how "wrong" we probably were for each other, the first three years of our marriage were good. The last seven have been pretty good, too. Those middle seven were miserable. I have written from those bad memories because someone is there *now*. I may be there again next week for a little while.

Point is, over the course of watching all that Divorce Court, it occurred to me that I wasn't alone in wondering whether I'd married the wrong guy, married too young, or if I was the only warm-blooded American wife who still hadn't quite figured out the whole sex thing even though I'd already given birth to a kid. In the midst of this growing revelation, I got comfortable with the idea that I wouldn't be enamored with Stevie every day (see chapter 6), and vice versa.

Even now, I continue learning to address my questions with biblical principles. I'm learning to get over myself and stay married to my first husband already.

There are many marriage books on the market today dealing with hot topics like infidelity, communication styles, addictions, abuse, and blended families/in-laws. This book doesn't attempt to tackle those well-covered issues that people can often find support groups for. Rather, this book deals with the smaller inklings that catch, snag, and slowly unravel the fabric of a marriage as we go about our day-to-day activities. Silently. It's my belief that the larger issues are often predicated by these smaller, mind-altering ponderings that should be nipped in the bud.

I'm here with the shears.

I pray that reading these true* anecdotes, retrospective lessons, and prayers will quiet the voices of discouragement in a wife's mind and open her heart to the hope of an imperfect, yet satisfying marriage that strengthens her walk with Christ.

Peace,
Michelle

* A few names have been changed to protect identities.

Chapter 1:
We Started Off Wrong

I'm sure our wedding picture could appear on posters warning romantic kids about what *not* to do. For starters, I was four months pregnant when we married. Stevie and I were in love, but I'd be lying if I said our unborn baby wasn't a major factor in our decision to marry after our thirteen-month long-distance courtship.

Stevie was twenty-three, I was twenty-one. He had a child from a previous relationship, and I was still secretly reeling from a past heartbreak. We both came from so-called "broken homes." His parents divorced when he was in middle school, mine when I was only a child, though my mother re-married when I was four. She and my step-father later divorced. Neither Stevie nor I had any kind of model for a successful marriage.

Stevie had said that he was raised in the church, but (as is turns out) we had two different working definitions of what it meant to be church-reared. He was a CME member (Christmas, Mother's Day, and Easter), while I was the child of the church musician (attending services every Sunday, many weeknights, too). Nonetheless, we were equally yoked because we were both spiritual infants. Probably more like spiritual embryos.

But we were in love. And Stevie had super-hot legs.

The one good thing was our financial situation. I had just finished college and begun making decent money as a teacher, while Stevie worked at a plastic manufacturing company. We had very little debt. Stevie was good with money, and we both really liked seventy-nine cent burritos.

As the "bad years" came upon our marriage, a slew of regrets constantly nagged me:

- *I wished I'd known him better before I'd gone and gotten myself pregnant.*
- *I wished I hadn't gotten myself pregnant in the first place.*
- *We shouldn't have married just because of the baby.*
- *We were too young—I barely even knew myself.*
- *We didn't have time to settle into our marriage before the baby got here.*
- *We should have had more than thirty minutes of pre-marital counseling.*
- *I should have checked his church attendance record.*

I imagined myself writing any or all of these statements on papers requesting a divorce. Who could expect us to overcome those feats? Why didn't anyone tell me how hard marriage could be?

To make my personal pity-party even worse, I was the first of my college friends to get married. Watching them move ahead and do all the things I wanted to do but couldn't, thanks to my brand-spankin'-new family, didn't help at all.

I didn't want a divorce. I didn't want to stay married. I just wished the whole thing had never happened.

* * * * *

Granted, I wouldn't want my daughter to marry under these circumstances. But if I had it to do over again, I wouldn't change anything for Stevie and me because the truth is: every marriage is a foreign land. Over these years that my husband and I have been together, I've seen young and old, rich and poor, pregnant and non-pregnant, Christian and non-believer, childhood friends and internet-matched couples rise and fall. Sometimes the people who think they've got it all together don't. Sometimes the ones who don't have a clue figure it out *together* and overcome all their previous folly, by the grace of God.

Whatever shoulda, woulda, couldas you have about marrying your husband when you did, let them go. Maybe you could have done better. You definitely could have done worse. You made a decision with the information you had at the time, and that's all anyone can do.

The beauty of a life surrendered to God is His willingness to intervene where His people fall short. If you recognize that your marriage began in a less-than-desirable state, talk to God about it. Admit your shortcomings and ask Him to make sense of your tangled mess. He has a way of un-raveling knots without breaking the string!

*****

Father, I repent of my willful disobedience, and I thank You for Your watchful eye where I was simply ignorant. You have preserved me and this marriage for Your purposes, and I want the testimony of Your ability to deliver us beyond our faults. In Jesus' Name, Amen.

Chapter 2:
I Think I Married the Wrong Guy

In the middle of our seven-year bad-marriage mayhem, I talked with a co-worker who'd been married about twenty-three years to a really great man. I honestly couldn't imagine a cuter, more perfect Christian couple. It appeared they had the kind of marriage I could have had if I'd stayed with this one particular guy I met at a Whodini and Grandmaster Flash rap concert.

It was the eighties, alright?

Anyway, I'd been watching my co-worker, thinking she was in this "perfect" marriage with "the one" who was made just for her. I mentally kicked myself because maybe I shouldn't have let concert-guy get away, or maybe I'd never meet "the one" since I was already married to the *un*-one.

My co-worker didn't know I was struggling in my marriage, but she was "good people," so I decided I'd pick her brain on one of those late Friday afternoons when everyone was sitting around the office waiting for the clock to strike quitin' time.

Somehow, I moseyed into the question, "Have you ever thought maybe you should have married someone else?"

She leaned forward and confessed, "There was this one guy in college, Bruce. He liked me and I liked him. I chose Phillip, but I have wondered what could have happened with me and Bruce."

Well, I wanted to know if Bruce was rich now, which would totally clear things up for me. But, of course, I had to dress up my inquiry a bit. "Have you seen Bruce since college? What's he up to?"

Her eyes twinkled slightly. "Yes. He was at our reunion. Still as handsome as ever. He's married, has kids, you know, a regular life."

Drats! Nothing spectacular. Just a regular guy with a regular life, much like the one she had with Phillip.

* * * * *

I left that conversation feeling she hadn't really helped me, but in retrospect, I realize this brief talk could be summarized in the advice I'd give any wife who's wondering if she married the wrong guy. Here goes: In all likelihood, there's probably a fairly large number of guys you could have married to arrive at a "regular" marriage much like the one you're in now. I know, I know, everyone wants to feel like there's just ONE super-guy out there who's a perfect match.

Step a-*waaaaaay* from the romance novel. No matter who you marry, half the marriage is already set because of you. Yes, *you* are going to show up in every relationship you have, so the other person can't possibly make *all* the difference. Who you married is, at most, only half the problem. Truth is: "The one" is whoever you make it work with.

Secondly, even if you believe you married the wrong guy, God is bigger than your mistakes and bad decisions. When He allows a less-than-perfect choice, He is willing and able to intervene upon sincere request.

* * * * *

Father, I trust You with my past as much as my present and my future. Whatever I did or didn't do, I give to You. Your ways are higher than mine and I trust You to make sense of my decisions. Cause me to see how You have always watched over me, even to this point of complete surrender. Thank You, God, for pulling me back to You. In Jesus' name, Amen.

Late-Breaking News (Chapter 2B)

Just YESTERDAY I got a Facebook friend request from concert-guy. (God just cracks me up sometimes.) Anyway, I friended him...took a look around his pages...all I can say is: The grass is NOT greener on the other side. It's brown, y'all. *Brown!*

I prayed for concert-guy, bless his heart.

Chapter 3:
I'm Just Not That Into Sex

Honestly, I thought about leaving this chapter out of the book. I'm no sex expert. But no marriage book is complete without some discussion of sex, especially since it's the only relationship where this physical expression of love is ordained. I'm guessing He knew marriage needed some extra perks! So, I'll throw in my two cents—with a pinky finger gently resting on the backspace key.

Several months ago, I was at a Christmas craft event when this lady approached my booth, and we somehow started talking about marriage. Within minutes, she blurted out, "We've got the usual problem."

My interest piqued. "What usual problem?" *Do I have this problem?*

"You knnnnnnow." She kind of winked at me and waited for her preschool-age daughter to wander off a bit, then whispered, "Sex."

"Oh." She had me now. Since we were total, complete strangers, I figured we might as well go there, right? "What's the deal? Don't you like it?"

"I like it, I just don't want to *do* it all the time." She went on to say that her husband pretty much wanted it every day. She, on the other hand, was too tired.

So I asked, "What do you do all day?" Seriously, she only had that one kid, and she was hanging out at a craft fair in the middle of the work week. To someone who juggled two kids born twenty months apart while working full-time as a public school teacher, I'm thinking, *She should have some energy left by the time her husband gets home from work.*

Turned out, she was a photographer with a flexible schedule.

"Okay, so why are you so tired every day?"

She shrugged. "I guess I'm not really *tired*, I just don't *feel* like doing it."

The more we talked, the more I realized her problem wasn't her husband. Her problem wasn't even sex, actually. It was a combination of communication, self-esteem, good-girls-don't issues that couldn't be fixed before her daughter broke something at the next vendor's booth.

I recommended a few good books to her (which I'll share later) and we exchanged cards, not that I ever expect to hear from her. It might be kind of hard to back into a nice, regular friendship at this point, I guess.

* * * * *

Our conversation brought up several thoughts about why and where we go wrong with sex. So, let's get real about this. If you're not on the same page with your husband sexually, there's a reason why. Whether the underlying issue is poor communication, baggage from the past, selfishness, too much stress, or a lack of understanding about your own physical anatomy, God has gifted us with His word and with other writers who have researched and reported the nitty-gritty of how you and your husband can experience a mutually satisfying sex life as your great marriage continues to blossom.

The only tip I have to share is this: Contrary to what all those romance novels and Lifetime movies portray, sex does not always have to be a huge production. A seasoned wife knows that in real life, we don't always have time for flower petals, hot baths, and hours of foreplay. Sometimes you just do it already. I mean, there's anniversary weekend getaway sex and then there's Tuesday-night-we-gotta-go-to-work-in-the-morning sex.

Even if you're not in the mood, concentrate on being your husband's dream lover. You just might get into it along the way. Sometimes sex is one of those things you didn't really know you wanted until you started doing it and then you're like, "Well, I'm sure glad I stayed up for that, good buddy."

When you are in a loving, caring, nurturing marriage, sex is a spiritually, emotionally, and physically satisfying experience. I wish you a rewarding, joyful sex life with your husband. And here are three books that I think can help you get there.

At one point, I had need of each of these books. Things are much better now, thank God. If you're suffering sexually, I hereby pass this blessed wisdom on to you.

- ***Intimate Issues: 21 Questions Christian Women Ask About Sex* by Linda Dillow and Lorraine Pintus**
  This book tackles some of the tough questions about sex with godly insight. I thought their concept of a "*soul*gasm" was very interesting. Some chapter titles to give you an idea: What's *not* okay in bed? What do I do when I don't want to do it? How can I make love with children wrapped around my knees? What's the big deal about orgasm?
- ***Becoming One* by Joe Beam**
  This book actually has a workbook that you and your husband can tackle together. This book deals more with how to get emotionally naked so that you can enjoy physical intimacy even more. My hubby didn't read the entire book, but I did, and it gave me insight into the male psyche.
- ***Sexplosion: A Biblically Based Sexual Intimacy Workshop for Wives* by Ramona Bailey**
  The basis for this book is scriptural, of course, but it's more of a how-to than the others I've recommended. If you have trouble experiencing sexual pleasure for reasons that you *don't* think are rooted in deep-seated

emotional or psychological problems, this book offers practical suggestions. Discover what works for you, and learn to speed up your sexual response. Lots of great homework assignments!

* * * * *

Father, thank You for the gift of sex. I submit to Your perfect will for my marriage, including physical intimacy. Show me how to give and receive this wonderful gift, and make our physical expressions of love and affection an ongoing reminder of all that is good and perfect in You. In Jesus' Name, Amen.

Chapter 4:
We've Grown Apart

Remember that little clause in the marriage vows: *for better or for worse?* If you're like me, you breezed past those words, thinking, "Yeah, get on with it already. How bad can it get? It only gets *really* bad for people who didn't really love each other in the first place, right?"

LOL!

I'm glad I can laugh now, because Thanksgiving evening, 1998, was our big "we've grown apart" conversation. We'd been married a little over five years, and I was totally through—ready to wash my hands of this whole thing and start my life over (with two kids and a mortgage). I knew I couldn't stay miserably married for the next fifty years. God was just gonna have to forgive me because I was throwing in the towel, folks.

The conversation went a little something like this:

"Steve, we need to talk."

"About what *now?*"

I took a deep breath. "About our marriage. I'm sorry to say this, but this will be our last Thanksgiving together as a family."

Stevie shook his head, sat down at the kitchen table next to me. "What's the problem *now*, Michelle?"

"I think it's pretty clear that neither of us is happy. We don't want the same things in life anymore."

"*You're* the one who's not happy," he stated. "I'm fine."

I continued, ignoring his observation and determined to convince him that we were, indeed, both very unhappy whether he realized it or not. "You've got your life and I've got mine."

He switched into male problem-solving mode. "Okay. Let's start doing more stuff together."

"That's not *it*." How could I explain that the *feeling* was gone? That I didn't *want* to do more stuff with him. I tried another angle. "It's like we're roommates."

"So what do you want me to do?"

I gave up. "I can't live like this anymore. I think we should go our separate ways."

"So what are you saying?" he asked.

"This is it."

He shrugged. "What?"

Did he really want me to say it? "The end."

"Okay, Michelle. If this is the way you want it." He sighed and got up from the table.

Of course, I followed him to the living room. "Don't blame it all on me!" I promptly ran through a list of his most recent transgressions. "We have to face facts. We've grown apart."

We went back and forth probably another five minutes. The heated discussion came to a screeching halt when he shattered my master plan, which was to stay in the house with the kids. I figured it would be traumatic enough for them to see their father leave. I didn't want to add losing their home on top of all the drama.

Anyway, Stevie busted my pre-packaged scheme with, "I'm not leaving this house."

Bewildered, I asked, "You want me and the kids to go find an apartment or something?"

"The kids can stay with me. If you want to leave, leave, but I'm staying in this house."

Flashbacks of *Kramer vs. Kramer* raced through my brain. Part of me was angry that Stevie wasn't doing things my way. Part of me was just really irked by the thought that someday, some other woman might live in this house, which I'd been wanting since I was 16 years old.

Foiled again, I resolved to stay married until I could come up with another scheme to take over the world...

* * * * *

I thank God Stevie put his foot down on the house thing. His refusal to follow through with my bright idea set up circumstances that forced both of us to face our issues head-on. Soon after, we enrolled in counseling and realized that every couple has seasons where one or both parties feel as though they're not exactly in sync. No reason to call the marriage quits.

Rearing kids, working outside of home, going back to school, caring for aging parents, joining a very active ministry, grieving the loss of a loved one—these are all events that can create space between husband and wife. These are also events we call...life.

God has a way of setting up experiences and circumstances that cause newlyweds to mature and develop into silver-haired lovebirds who occasionally screech at one another. Love rolls with life (1 Corinthians 13:4-7). Trust that He is developing His love in both of you within the divine confines of holy matrimony.

* * * * *

Father, it appears that my husband and I are leading separate lives. Things aren't looking too good. Thank You for assuring me that present conditions don't dictate our future. Restore my heart to You and to my husband, and teach us how to practice Your love in this marriage. In Jesus' Holy name, Amen.

Chapter 5:
I Miss the Thrill of Being Single

Who doesn't miss giddy blind dates and stepping into every Wal-Mart feeling like today might be the day you meet *him*? Each stop at the gas pump could lead to true love. Gives you a reason to comb your hair every day, you know?

The single life was, for some of us, pretty exciting (or we like to think it was). New adventures every weekend, free dinners, free movies, lots of time to hang with the girls. And what were we hoping for? What we've got now—the stable, consistent, married life.

Hmm…what's wrong with this picture? I ran around hoping I'd meet someone to settle down with, but now that I had him, I kinda wished I was still looking for my prince in anything-can-happen land.

Reminds me of the story of the middle-aged guy who finally got the Porsche he'd been wanting since he was a teenager. Someone asked, "So what was the best day ever with this Porsche?"

The man replied, "The day before I got it."

* * * * *

Everything loses its novelty after a while. This is true of cars, puppies, people, and, sadly, leopard print boots.

Married life can seem especially boring when your friends are still single, enjoying the rush of new possibilities and bragging about all their choices. "Oh my gosh, I met this new guy! He's so cute!" *Blah, blah, blah*. It's hard to be happy for them when you're secretly jealous of their lives because you've discovered that marriage can be like that high-maintenance, high-priced Porsche.

It's okay to remember the single days fondly. I also miss the pre-kid days, when I could come home from McDonalds and eat my very own McNuggets in peace. Alas, this comes with "Mommy" territory.

Welcome to what we call "seasons" in a woman's life. King Solomon wisely noted that there is a season for all things (Ecclesiastes 3:1-8). Transitioning from one stage in life to the next can bring a sense of sadness or loss for the person you used to be. If you're blessed to live a long life on earth, you'll experience many seasons and learn how to live each one to the fullest, carrying the best memories and lessons into the next season. No worries, no looking back.

Acknowledge to God in prayer that you feel sad, but don't let your feelings have the last word. Wait in His presence for His comfort. He "gets" you, even in these areas that you'd rather not admit to anyone, which is precisely what makes Him your all-season BFF.

* * * * *

Heavenly Father, I thank You for the fond memories of the previous season, and for this new season You have ordained for me. Help me embrace the changes in my life so I can enjoy my marriage and enjoy my relationship with You each day. In Jesus' name, Amen.

Chapter 6:
I Love my Husband, but I'm Not In Love
or
I Love My Husband, but I Don't Like Him
or
I Don't Even Like My Husband Today

One of the things that totally endeared me to Stevie when we were dating was his sense of humor. Being around him made me think of my dad, who could keep a room full of people laughing. Stevie totally cracked me up with his little observations, like when he said that my big toe nail resembled a garage door. Who *wouldn't* fall in love with this man?

Our first months of marriage were absolutely wonderful. I took joy in lowering the toilet seat. After all, this was the way of men. We laughed about our differences (he puts water in ketchup and shampoo to make them last longer). Soon after, our son was born, and I giggled inside at my husband's fear of holding our precious baby.

Fast-forward a few years. All it takes is one good time to fall bottom-first into a toilet bowl while your hair is only half-clean from diluted shampoo to change your mind about what you find attractive about your husband. *And why on earth is he calling me from the kitchen to comfort a crying toddler who's two feet away from him?*

Nothing Stevie said could be funny at that point. In fact, his odd little commentaries and carefree behavior annoyed me.

Nonetheless, this is the husband I chose. For better or for worse.

* * * * *

Every relationship loses its innocence at some point. Learning to love someone for the long haul means understanding that some days, you may roll over, look at your husband's face, and think to yourself, "I'm not feeling him today, but I choose to keep loving him anyway." Your feelings can be manipulated by what you decide.

As your rosy-colored view of your hubby fades—and, imagine this, his view of you will morph, too—what you're both left with is a commitment and your faith in God to see this whole thing through.

Some days are better than others, I'll give you that. But please don't put so much pressure on yourself or your husband to "feel" in love. Nobody "feels" in love all the time.

I was talking to the married ladies in my book club last week and we came up with this totally unscientific, eight-Christian-ladies-chatting rule: If you're "in love" with your husband 70% of the time, you're doing well. That leaves two days a week to feel out-of-love and still be okay. Plus, it's a "C" grade; passing. Forget the honor roll. Marriage is one area where expecting straight A's will lead to certain failure.

Be at peace with some degree of imperfection in your marriage and realize that God's grace and His word stands even on those days when your feelings don't line up with your commitment.

* * * * *

Lord, I thank You for loving me 100% of the time. God, I love my husband, but right now, I'm not feeling the love. Thank You for the authority of Your word, and I ask You to take control of my emotions and restore my peace.

Chapter 7:
We've Got Parenting Issues

The Stimpsons and the Musics (my childhood family) apparently had very different households, and neither of them was completely right (to put it nicely).

In Stevie's parents' household, there was plenty of cussing. I suppose I should give some credit and say at least the parents did the cussing, not the children—but I really don't know if that's any better. One of the first times Stevie and I really had it out (I mean O-U-T) was when he got angry at our young son and said a curse word while fussing at my baby. I totally, completely flipped! I laid into Stevie like Mamma Bear on steroids because in my world, adults did not cuss at children. Smart-mouthed teenagers were probably fair game, but never little kids.

By the time Stevie and I finished arguing, I'd said a few choice words of my own and threatened to call Child Protective Services on him if he ever cursed at either of our kids again.

Later, when we talked about the incident, Stevie said, "Cussing is a part of life." His parents cussed, lots of parents cussed, and he didn't see it as a huge problem.

I disagreed wholeheartedly.

I brought in my fair share of ungodly parenting expectations, too. Though a licensed educator and proponent of peace, I dutifully forewarned our son about his first fight, explaining exactly what to do when he got sent to the principal's office. Not *if* a fight occurred, but *when*. "You tell the principal he'd better not paddle you until he calls me first," I counseled.

By the time Steven got to fifth grade and still hadn't had a fight, I began to worry. After all, I figured no childhood was complete without at least one good playground brawl. This boy was about to go to middle school unprepared. *Where did I go wrong?*

I blamed Stevie for this lack of aggression in our son. If he'd taken him to a football game or two, taught him how to box, or at least wrestled with him in the den, Steven would have had the fight by now! Stevie, on the other hand, said it was no big deal; Steven liked video games and we should leave him alone.

* * * * *

Stevie and I still disagree about many things when it comes to the children. My good friend Jayne, whose children have been out of their home for five years, says there's much more peace in an empty nest. I'm counting down the days.

Careful study of the scriptures revealed that both Stevie and I were taught incorrectly about many things as children. Traditions, expectations, and even superstitions were guiding our beliefs rather than the word of God. I marvel at how well our kids are doing in spite of us!

If you and your husband disagree on how to raise the children, search the scriptures to find the heart of God, and take the matter before Him in prayer. Children are precious to Jesus (Mark 10:14). Renounce the ungodly patterns that you and/or your husband might have experienced growing up, and confess the will of God for your family. Watch God intervene. And trust that He will graciously shield your children and soften their memories where you and your husband miss the mark.

* * * * *

Father, You love children because they have such tender hearts. Make me tender-hearted, Lord, so that I can intercede for my family. Show me when to stand firm on Your word and when to compromise where human differences clash. Teach my husband and me to be godly parents so that we can add to the Kingdom with the children you have placed in our care. In Jesus' Name, Amen.

Chapter 8:
I Feel Trapped

Nothing's worse than feeling like you're stuck in a relationship you can't escape because of kids, financial obligations, fear of embarrassment, or just plain old fear itself. I remember sitting down one day calculating how long it would be before my kids finished high school, figuring how much money I needed to pilfer between then and now so I could make a clean break. [Y'all, I still don't understand why I was so dead-set on sabotaging my marriage. I only hope women will learn from my foolishness!]

Somewhere in this crisis, I called my grandmother, who was married more than fifty years to my late grandpa. My grandmother is a feisty woman who left secretarial school against her parents' wishes in order to marry my grandfather and promptly gave birth to eight children. In the early years of my grandparents' marriage, my grandfather was…well…let's just say he was a juke-joint-piano-playin', whiskey-drinkin' rascal.

My grandmother, a church-goin' woman, tolerated his sinful ways for many years before he gave his life to Christ and became a loving pastor.

I guess I figured if there was anyone who knew how to stay "trapped" indefinitely, Grandma would be the one.

So, I'm like, "Grandma, I know all these women in your generation stayed married for fifty and sixty years, but I want you to tell me the truth. Did y'all stay married because you *wanted* to or because you *had* to?" I go on to insinuate that, at some level, she and all the women in her circle were trapped. Really, where were they gonna go with all those kids and no education? No vocational skills? Not to mention being a woman of color in the 1950's south.

Before I got too carried away, she cut me off. "Mickey"—that's my nickname—"let me tell you something. There's a few folks I think shouldn'ta stayed married, 'specially women with beatin'-type husbands, but the rest of us stayed married 'cause *we told God* we would and that's all there is to it. A covenant is a covenant, don't matter what year it is."

"Okay, Grandma. I gotta go now."

* * * * *

Now that Grandma has settled the covenant issue, let's just concede that you and I are indeed "trapped" and have been since the day we married our husbands. Only, back then, it was more like...love-locked. What's the difference? Our attitudes.

Honoring our commitments to God should bring tremendous joy and hope into our lives, not everlasting dread. When following the will of God is a
burdensome chore, I find that an open, honest prayer to God is the best way to lay it all out on the table and release resentment so that He can restore me to the right perspective.

* * * * *

God, I feel totally trapped in this marriage. If it weren't for the circumstances, I would have left already. I thank You for circumstances that cause me to pause and re-consider the covenant. You work all things for the good of those who love You. Lord, I ask you to change my perspective on this marriage. Line me up with Your word, for the sake of Your glory. And thank You for trapping me in Your eternal love. In Jesus' name, Amen.

Chapter 9:
This Submission Thing is Ridiculous

When I was twelve years old, a preacher came to our church to conduct a revival. My mother, as usual, made me get in the prayer line under the adage, "You never turn down prayer." So, there I was at the altar wearing this pre-teen attitude, bubbling with resentment. The minister put his hand on my forehead and began praying for me. When I failed to break out in tears, he pronounced to my mother and everyone in the church that I had a "spirit of rebellion" on me.

I was actually quite proud of the label. I returned to my seat hoping my mother would remember this declaration the next time she had an inclination to force me down the aisle.

Fast forward nine years. I'm at that same church exchanging vows with my husband. When we get to the "obey" part of the vows, I repeat the minister's words, but I'm haunted by the day the preacher labeled me rebellious at this very same altar. I thought, *That other preacher was right. I really don't want to obey my husband, but if I don't repeat the words, the minister probably won't marry us, and my mom will want her money back for the candelabra.*

So, by virtue of traditional wedding vows, I agreed to be submissive as part of the deal, but had no intention of following through. Nor did I think I could actually be held liable for submission, seeing as a state-licensed preacher had already declared me rebellious.

I bucked on just about everything when we first got married. I'd been raised to go to college and get a good job so I would never have to depend on a man. I thought the pinnacle of adulthood was to be a strong, independent woman who could stand on her own two feet. My heroines didn't take no stuff from men. They were smart-talking, bold, quick-witted women with even quicker tongues. They were also mostly single or unhappily married, mind you, but I looked up to them nonetheless. I was clueless about the power of submission to God or my husband.

The first time I can actually remember giving in to Stevie's way of doing things was when my daughter started pre-school. I wanted her dressed a certain way (i.e., matching and neat), but since I was up and out of the house with our son before Stevie would leave with our daughter a few hours later, I lost control of the situation. Stevie let our three-year-old dress herself in whatever she wanted to wear to school, despite what I might have laid out the night before.

My daughter looked a hot mess when I picked her up from daycare in the evenings.

The result of my surrender, however, was a pretty self-confident three-year-old who taught herself to tie her own shoes. My poor son, who was five at the
time, hadn't even gotten the opportunity to *try* tying his shoes because I was still doing it for him.

My daughter's teacher was so thankful, she told me, "It's so nice to have someone else around who can tie shoes!"

Never mind the plaid shirt and paisley pants. That girl could make bunny ears!

* * * * *

Submission is not about giving my husband biblical permission to mistreat me or even saying that he's always right. Respecting, honoring, and submitting to Stevie in everything that's not outside God's will is a matter of trusting that when God set this whole marriage thing up, He knew what He was doing. This epic battle of my will versus God's does not always go well in the Stimpson household, and I realize there are biblical parameters both husband and wife need to respect with regard to godly submission.

But every time I see my daughter put on a pair of gym shoes (in the car, mind you, since she's always running late), I'm reminded of how much better things can turn out when I relinquish control and submit to my husband's way of doing things, even when I disagree.

Submitting to our husbands gives God perfect permission to steer and direct our families toward His perfect plan.

* * * * *

Father, I repent of allowing rebellion to guide me rather than Your Holy Spirit. Teach me how to be respectful and submissive to those You have given authority over me, and help me to be compassionate and responsible where You have given me authority as well.

Chapter 10:
He's Not Who I Thought He Was

Here's a list of some things I wish I had known about Stevie before we got married:

- It takes him about an hour to really wake up in the mornings.
- He thinks having good manners means acting fake.
- He would rather change clothes than lose money by adjusting the thermostat.
- He thinks farting is funny.

Here's a list of some stuff I didn't tell Stevie about myself before we got married that he probably would liked to have known:

- I'm a last-minute person.
- I'm a night owl.

- I don't like cooking or cleaning.
- My neck has this weird hump that I kept covered with my hair while we dated.

I'm sure that's just the tip of the iceberg for both of us. Would I have married Stevie if I'd know these things? Probably. I like to think he would have married me, too.

Nobody's perfect, and everybody puts that best foot forward while dating. Even if you were around your husband almost 24/7 before you married, people change once the escape hatch is shut. People change with maturity. People change under pressure. Even if people don't change, your perspective of them will change over time once you get to know them intimately.

Let me assure you, you're not the first woman to feel she's gotten herself into a Jekyll and Hyde situation. If you feel your husband is suffering from mental illness, you need discernment from God on how to press for his healing. It's not normal for a man to suddenly start behaving violently or make an abrupt 180-degree change. Mental illness is healable, by the way, and God has many avenues through which to bring healing and wholeness.

On the other hand, some of us had clues about our husbands' kinks before we married. We just overlooked the slight irregularities because we were in love.

So, here you are married to a man you feel you hardly know. What are you supposed to do now? I say get to know the new him—your *real* husband who was cleverly disguised as Mr. Right before you walked down the aisle. I know, I know. You feel cheated. Dooped.

I'm praying that you will put your feelings and fantasies aside and deal with the reality. You're married to this guy and you both have to figure out how to make this work. None of us got a risk-free, money-back guarantee when we got married. We *all* came into this deal "as-is." And now, we're *all* busy forgiving, loving, laughing, crying, and forgiving *again* and *again* until death do us part which, basically, means every day.

The advice shared in Chapter 1 bears repeating here: Give all your shoulda, woulda, coulda's to the One who has watched over you all the days of your life. Rest assured that He knows the man you married, and He has allowed you to be the helpmate for your husband. It appears some husbands need more help than others. That's okay. This marriage is just the thing God will use to show you the true meaning of love.

* * * * *

Father, thank You for looking beyond all my faults and seeing my needs. Help me to perform this same act of love with my husband. Give me discernment about how to help my husband be the man You have called Him to be, for Your glory. In Jesus' Name, Amen.

Chapter 11:
I Can't Tolerate This Snoring Anymore!

It is with a somber face and complete sincerity that I dedicate an entire chapter of this book to the problem of snoring. Yes, I know there are dozens of things a person can do to irritate one's spouse. But this snoring takes the cake for me—or at least it used to.

Once, when Stevie and I were dating, we were at his parents' house watching television in the living room, which is about 35 feet away from the hallway leading to the bedrooms. As we watched television, I heard this loud, grating sound emanating from one of the rooms. And yet, my then-boyfriend kept watching television as though he didn't hear this noise.

Well, I didn't want to be rude, but this mysterious racket was getting so loud, I almost couldn't hear the TV. So, I asked, "Why is your brother in his room roaring?" I seriously thought maybe his brother was in there practicing for a role in a play or something.

Stevie replied, "That's not my brother. That's my dad. Snoring."

I had never heard anyone in my life snore like that! I didn't even know it was possible to snore so loudly that other people in other rooms of a house could *feel* it. Annoyed, I asked Stevie if we could leave. Little did I know, months later I'd find out that the snoring apple doesn't fall far from the tree!

This is hard to even write, but I'll admit: For the first eight years of our marriage, Stevie and I rarely slept in the same bed at night. We might have started off in the same bed, but at some point during the night, one of us would have to leave.

I resented Stevie for snoring; he resented me waking him up in the middle of the night. He accused me of waking him up for no reason; I accused him of being an exceptionally obnoxious snorer. I even recorded him snoring once so he could hear how loud he was. He said I probably had the volume up too high, plus it wasn't his fault I was a light sleeper.

Stevie tried nose strips, but they wouldn't stick because his nose sweats at night. He also tried some contraption that set his jaw differently, but he said it was uncomfortable. I tried earplugs, but they didn't stop the bonus snoring vibration effect. Sometimes, I took Nyquil to knock myself out. The Nyquil did work, but then there's the whole drugging-myself thing, which I gathered probably wasn't a good long-term plan.

After nearly a decade of this midnight bed-shuffle, I was talking to a newlywed girlfriend of mine and confessed our weird sleeping arrangements. She said, "Y'all gotta do something, girl. That's not normal. It's got to be affecting your marriage."

Lightbulb moment. I had never considered the fact that arguing in the middle of the night followed by
sleeping in separate beds might be impacting our marriage. *Duh!* Still, I didn't know what to do about it.

Somehow, some way, it occurred to me to pray about the situation. But what was I supposed to pray? *God help my husband stop snoring? God make me sleep like a drunk person?* Was this whole thing somebody's fault? Was there a scripture on snoring? Though I was unclear of what to pray, I took the matter before God in a jumble of confused words. Thank God He knows how to make sense of our confusion.

I can't tell you exactly when God changed the situation, but He did. One morning, I woke up in my bed next to my husband and thought, *That's weird. We slept in the same bed together all night, and I didn't even have to tell him to turn over.* And then it happened again the next morning. The next night, one of us left the bedroom because of snoring. But then on morning four, I was still in my bed next to Stevie. Before I knew it, God had changed the situation. I'm not sure whether He lowered the volume on Stevie's snoring or if He made my ears less sensitive to it. I wish I could explain exactly what happened—especially since this is an informational book and all—but I can't. I just know He did *something* to fix the situation.

* * * * *

No matter if the problem is snoring, annoying habits, or pesky characteristics, God has a way of fixing things. He may fix your husband, He may fix the way your respond to your husband, or He may be fixing something in you that can only be addressed by continually chipping away the old you. Trust Him to create the best resolution in practical matters. No job is too big, small, or loud for Him!

* * * * *

Father, thank You for caring about me so deeply. I'm glad to know I can come to you with everything that concerns me. Show me where my life may be out of line with Your will. I place full confidence in Your ability to handle me and the people around me so that, in the end, Your name will be glorified. In Jesus' name, Amen.

Late-Breaking News (Chapter 11B)

Now Stevie says I snore. He says he's going to record me on his cell phone. We'll see…

Chapter 12:
I Don't Think I Can Do This Domestic Stuff

Jiffy Cornbread Mix is perhaps the simplest recipe on the planet. One package of mix, one egg, one-third cup of milk. Blend all that, pour in a greased pan, and bake for 15 minutes at 400 degrees.

Should be easy, right? Not for me. I've messed up on Jiffy Cornbread. Twice. I've also messed up laundry and the sink incinerator, and I didn't even know you're supposed to vacuum baseboards with a different attachment.

Let me explain. My mom was a nurse. She worked odd hours, which meant a lot of sandwiches and pizza when I was growing up. When I was twelve years old, she was involved in a major car accident, and I became the "mother" of the family for several years. More sandwiches, more pizza, less cleaning up. It was pretty much every man for himself. Consequently, becoming a wife years later posed serious issues for me.

I didn't know how to plan meals or set up a laundry routine. I didn't know how to run a household. I still don't. I stand in awe of domestic goddesses who have trained their kids to prefer apples over chips, whose labels face forward in the cupboard, and whose towels are folded with the stripe on the right. Or is it the left?

Either way, that's not me, and Stevie was very disappointed to find that he'd married a church-goin'-girl who didn't abide by the clichés that the way to a man's heart is through his stomach, or cleanliness is next to godliness.

Our apartment was always a wreck, especially with a newborn. When we moved into our house, I did slightly better. Thank God the kids got old enough to take on some of the chores. My son started folding towels when he was four, and my daughter is the princess of organization. Plus, my dog eats any scraps that fall on the floor. I have no idea what I'm going to do when all this help is gone!

* * * * *

If you're feeling inadequate or overwhelmed by your domestic responsibilities, consider my two-part advice. First, understand there's no one right way to run a household. If you're not a great cook, find simple recipes that your family enjoys and roll with it. Leave the fancy, gourmet stuff to the experts at Chili's. I've wasted so much money on botched meal creations, my husband has actually asked me to stop experimenting and stick to what I know. It's okay.

I also hold to a pretty strict no-dropping-by-unannounced rule. We don't have one of those hardly-touched, formal living areas in our home, so there's always a good five or ten minutes worth of straightening up to do before company comes over. It is what it is, you know?

Secondly, get help! When I was in graduate school and working full time, there was no way I could juggle all those plates at once. We hired a housekeeper who came twice a month during that season of our lives. I've also found that if I ask Stevie to do just one or two very specific things, he will do them. He is actually a very gifted vacuummer.

It's okay to get help from God, too. If you truly hate cooking, cleaning, and all things domestic, pray. Tell God that you resent the fact that *every single day* the bed needs to be made and no matter how much dusting you do, the dust eventually returns. Ask Him to change what needs to be changed in you and show you how to make all this work to His satisfaction.

* * * * *

Father, thank You for entrusting me with a responsibility to my family and to the shelter You have provided for us. I desire to please You with every aspect of my life. Give me the discipline to carry out my responsibilities to You and my husband, and the grace to get over things that don't matter one way or the other. In Jesus' name, Amen.

Chapter 13:
Watching My Parents Messed Me Up

No one ever told me what to look for in a husband or how a godly marriage was supposed to operate. At the tender age of 17, my fantasy about marriage went a little something like this...

I'm at home on a Saturday night. My husband is out partying at a night club while the kids and I are watching movies. They don't ask where Daddy is. They already know not to expect him home on a Saturday night. After the movie, I tell the kids to take their baths while I lay out their clothes for Sunday morning service. I kiss the kids good night.

Sometime around two in the morning, my husband stumbles into the house sloppy drunk. He's boisterous, he's delirious, but all he can think about is how much he wants me because none of those loose, wild women at the club can compare to me. We make mad, passionate love, and he snoozes off to sleep. I gingerly touch his forehead and pray, "God, please change my husband." I drift off to dreamland, happy that my husband always comes home to me.

The next morning, the children and I get up early. My husband is still too drunk to get out of bed, but he does tell me how nice I look, and he gives the kids a few quarters for offering. The kids and I go off to church, where I continue to pray that God will someday save my husband's soul.

About fifty years later, my husband walks down the center church aisle and gives his life to Christ. It's the most joyous day of my life, and it happened because I stuck with my husband and prayed this heathen over to the Lord's side.

Because I grew up witnessing a spiritually dysfunctional marriage, even my daydreams about my future husband were out of whack!

A few months after I got married, I remember talking to my mother and a friend of hers who was also in one of these church-girl-hooked-up-with-rascal type marriages. I'm sure the Holy Spirit took full control of my mouth the moment I declared to both of them, "Stevie and I are going to break this mold for crazy marriages."

One of them remarked, "I didn't know it was a mold."

* * * * *

Yes, it was a mold. A distorted, ungodly, generational mold that set me up for a bad marriage from the get-go.

Nonetheless, we can't blame our parents for our choices. Parents are people, too. They walk in the light they have at any given point in life, the same as you and I do every day. The good news is: You can get more light!

Allow God to illuminate the areas that have been darkened by generations of dysfunction in your family. Whether it was past rebellion, habits, or plain old ignorance, Jesus came to release us from those bondages and reveal His way of operating (John 10:10). Sin is broken! No matter what happened or didn't happen with your parents, His fantasy for your marriage can become your reality, thereby setting a new mold for future generations.

* * * * *

Father, I admit that I don't really know what a godly marriage looks like. I forgive anyone who has influenced me negatively, and I pray for their peace. I break every curse that has been set against my family by the blood of Jesus. I submit all previously held beliefs to the authority of Your word. Show me how to walk in Your promises and create a higher standard for generations to come. In Jesus' name, Amen.

Chapter 14:
Sometimes, He's Just Lazy

My grandmother told me once that a woman can work through *anything* with her husband so long as brought home a paycheck. Infidelity, abuse, alcoholism—all of those were problems that could be overcome. But when an able-bodied man's "just plain ol' sorry," it was time to move on, in her book.

That's the gospel according to Grandma Ruth (and probably Michelle, too). Yet, we have His book as our ultimate guide which, I know for a fact, has saved countless marriages.

The Stimpsons have had our fair share of husbandly unemployment. Stevie used to own a trucking company. When he made the transition from trucking to less taxing and (we hoped) more profitable work, he found himself unemployed at the beginning of the country's economic slump. For months, Stevie looked high and low for jobs but couldn't find anything. So, after a while, he just stopped looking.

Well, for the record, he *claimed* he was still completing applications online, but I didn't see any evidence of this alleged job search.

Frustration set in on my end. Stevie had always been a hard worker—which is one quality that attracted me to him. Now, that was gone.

We began arguing about what I perceived as his lack of tenacity. The money in our savings account was quickly dwindling, which added another layer of tension. I was repeatedly enraged when I came home from work and saw him lying on the couch still in his PJ's playing Madden football online against other grown men who, apparently, had nothing to do all day. *Where do they find these people?* Not to mention the house was a mess and there was no dinner on the stove.

After about six months of these shenanigans, I gave Stevie an ultimatum to get a job within two months or go move in with his mom until he found work because I could do bad all by myself. (Isn't it amazing how many worldly clichés we accept as truth?)

In the middle of all this chaos, I shared my situation with my prayerful writing critique partners. I asked them to pray that Stevie got a job because if he didn't, I was kicking him out.

I thank God for the women's wisdom in the midst of my temporary rebellion, a.k.a. sin. They prayed for Stevie for about ten seconds and then delved into praying for me. *Me?!* They asked God to give me patience, love, and understanding during this difficult time. Not exactly what I'd asked for, but certainly what I needed.

As my heart softened and I followed the women's example in prayer, God began to show me that Stevie wanted to work, but he was falling into depression about not being able to find a job quickly. I realized that if I didn't stand with and for my husband in prayer, the enemy was going to use unemployment to tear our family apart.

This wasn't about the job or the money. The enemy was simply attacking my marriage from a different angle, trying to take us back to the *old* us.

Instead of fussing at my husband, I started asking Stevie how I could be of service in helping him get a job. I made copies of his license and social security card, used my literary skills to spruce up his resume. I became his secretary and his number one cheerleader. When Stevie saw that I had begun to believe in him again, he got with the program and God blessed our family with steady employment for Stevie.

God did this for the Stimpsons. I have no reason to doubt He will align your family with His perfect will as well.

* * * * *

Now, let's lay down a foundation here. It's unbiblical for a man who's perfectly capable of providing for his family to refuse to work. When a man won't work, refuses to look for work, sabotages work opportunities, doesn't have a heart to work, he is out of line with God's perfect will. Men who don't work aren't supposed to eat (2 Thessalonians 3:10). Far be it from you or me to override that principal.

Actually, no one (male or female) is supposed to be here just lazyin' around and chillin'. Even if we had all the money we'd ever need sitting in an investment account drawing enough interest to meet our daily needs without ever touching the principal, we're still called to be productive with our lives.

But we shouldn't make the mistake of using God's will to beat others down. If your husband currently won't work, ask God to give you discernment about what's going on in his head. Give your husband the benefit of a doubt. Men created in God's image aren't *born* just plain ol' sorry.

Is your husband depressed? Does he feel under-qualified? Has God ordained this as a season for him to return to school or start the ministry he's been putting off? Does he feel that his financial contribution isn't necessary or appreciated? Furthermore, ask God to show you what (if anything) you can do to be a part of the solution. Most assuredly, prayer will be part of the answer.

* * * * *

Father, I thank You for being the ultimate provider, and thank You for making my husband a part of Your plan to be an avenue for Your provision. Show me how to pray for my husband. Line up employment that will be satisfying for him. Use me in Your perfect will for our family and make us faithful to use the increase for Your glory. In Jesus' name, Amen.

Chapter 15:
What Am I Supposed to Do Now?

I hope this book has compelled to reach to the One who wants to provide comfort and relief for your situation. Cast your cares—even the ones you'd rather not admit—on Him (1 Peter 5:7). Know that He's been reading right along with you, hoping first and foremost that You will turn to Him first as the true lover of your soul. Secondly, that you will give Him a chance to demonstrate how He works all things together for the good of those who love Him (Romans 8:28).

In closing, I leave you with four points that will, prayerfully, strengthen your walk with Christ and improve your marriage via improving you. I know, I know. You're tired of always being the one to offer the olive branch; the one who takes the high road. You wanna take the low road (wherever that is) every now and then. I mean, wouldn't it be nice if your husband or your boss or your kid came to you and said, "I was completely wrong. You were right. What can we do to move past this problem?"

Don't hold your breath.

You know what the Bible calls someone like you? A child of God. "Blessed are the peacemakers, for they will be called the children of God" (Matthew 5:9). Yep, that's you. A blessed child of God. It's hard being you, but somebody's got do it.

A while back, I was visiting an elementary school, talking to the kids about what it's like to be an author. One of the kids asked, "Is it hard to write a book?"

I thought about the question. As much as I love writing and enjoy the honor of being an author, there's something tremendously challenging about opening a blank Microsoft Word file and knowing that I need to fill all that white space with words. So, after pondering the child's question, I replied truthfully, "Yes, it is hard sometimes."

He shook his head and said, "I ain't writin' no book, then."

He wasn't willing to do a "hard" thing, but, hey, at

least he was honest about it. Who knows, maybe he'll grow up to be a…hmm…I can't think of any occupation I'd speak upon a child that doesn't require some degree of hard work.

The difference between the very natural task of gaining employment and the priceless spiritual revelations God has for His children brings us to (drum roll, please)…

Thing You Have to Know #1:
Following the Plan of God is Hard or as Easy as We Make It

Here's God's plan: we read something in the Bible or hear a sermon, the Spirit highlights phrases and words or adds special insight, we become a doer of the word, then our lives line up with the word. It's supposed to be that simple.

So why is it so *hard* for you? For me, too?

It's only hard because we resist. The moment we surrender and say, "Okay, God, if You say so, then it *is* so," and we act in faith, everything changes—starting in the spiritual realm, continuing into the natural realm.

The sooner, the more thoroughly, the more readily we give up our ways for God's way, the easier the changes will come. God will take us as far, as deep, and as fast as we will allow Him. Resistance and rebellion, however, simply delay development.

I thoroughly believe that God loves it when people get out of the way so He can do His thing! But who are these people denying His hand? Don't they know that He cares for them? Don't they love Him, too?

No. They don't. They can't, because they're dead. Enter...

Thing You Have to Know #2: There is No Evil Twin Living Inside You

I thank God for Steve McVey's book, *The Grace Walk Experience*, which does a wonderful job of discussing Paul's infamous why-do-I-do-what-I-don't-want-to-do angst (Romans 7) concerning why he does things he doesn't want to do, doesn't do what he needs to do. Really, who hasn't found herself in that predicament? I just lost a struggle with a piece of leftover Thanksgiving Day sweet potato pie this morning–I can relate!

But Paul goes on to say (Romans 8) that life in the Spirit overcomes the sin that lived inside his body before Christ.

Perhaps the most telling verse in this revelation is Colossians 3:3, *"For you died, and your life is now hidden with Christ in God."* The old you is dead. So, then, who is this chick whispering bad things to you – telling you that your marriage is a joke? She's the "default" you–the *you* who needs to be re-programmed by the renewing of your mind (Romans 12:2).

If you've got a default printer set on your computer, every time you print, the job will go to the printer you've designated as the "default" *unless* you choose otherwise. Life in Christ makes *Christ* our default. The old printer may try to pop up on the screen, but once we've chosen to make Christ our default mind (1 Cor. 2:16), we're not bound to the old way of life.

Furthermore, that chick isn't actually the old you talking (she's dead, remember). Satan has a way of disguising his voice as *your* voice, talking to you in first person, tricking you into thinking the old you—who is dead, capiche?—still has some kind of power over you. But she doesn't because…she's, uh, DEAD, thanks to Jesus!

Yes, you remember her, you saw the things she saw, you experienced what she experienced, you have memories of how she lived her life. But that doesn't mean she's still alive. Don't let dead things keep you from living. You live your life in Christ with God *now*.

Thing You Must Know #3: Start Where You Are, Stay in the Word

Let's say that last section just went over your head. (Don't feel bad, it happened to me, and I had a much better explanation than I gave you.) Nonetheless, if you come across something in this book or in the Bible that you don't understand or you just can't wrap your mind around, stop and ask the Holy Spirit for revelation.

I'm just one person sitting in front of a computer screen. I only know in part, but the Holy Spirit, the Spirit of God (1 Corinthians 2:11) is here to guide us into all truth (John 16:13) and make things known to us what we cannot know outside of the Holy Spirit, so ask for revelation. He'll give it to you. How do you know He will? Because He said He would (1 Corinthians 2: 6-16), and His integrity is unquestionable.

Or let's say you read something in the word that's extremely hard to believe given your experience and your entire family's track-record. Don't just mentally assent to what the Word says. Ask God to make His word true, experientially, for you.

In either case, just be honest before God. So much of what God wants to reveal to you isn't quantitative or objective. You will only know it when you know it, and the only way to know it is by Him. That's not bad news – that's good news. The truth is hidden *for* you, not *from* you, and God reveals Himself to those who seek Him (1 Corinthians 2:7)).

Even now, as I'm sitting in my local Panera restaurant writing these words, I realize this is like trying to *tell* you how to ride a bike. No matter how many bike-riding conferences you attend, you won't know how to roll for yourself until you get on that 10-speed and experience keeping balance while steering the front wheel. You can't know how to ride a bike any other way than to just *ride* it.

Thing You Must Know #4: When to Shut Up

I tried to come up with a nice little segue for this point, but there's no nice way to tell a woman to be quiet.

A wise woman understands the power of her words. She realizes that she will have what she says (Proverbs 18:21) and that what she has now is a culmination of what she has said to herself (Proverbs 23:7) and the words that have left her lips up until this point.

So, at a minimum, here are the when-to-shut-up ground rules:

1. **No nagging.** Period. If nagging worked, all husbands and children would be perfect.
2. **Don't slander your husband or your marriage.** Only share concerns about your husband/marriage with people who are part of the solution. If you feel you must vent, vent to God. He's a much better listener, and

He's actually in a position to do something about your concerns.

3. **Limit Conversations.** Too much talking leads to words that don't need to be spoken; i.e. sin (Proverbs 10:19). Following this rule will help with rules one and two.

4. **Don't attend pity-parties (yours or anyone else's).** When you're tempted to go into woe-is-me mode either verbally or internally, stop, drop, and pray – or sing a praise song or go watch *The Flintstones* or something. You simply *cannot* allow the spirit of grumbling and complaining to take over you.

A truly spiritual wife probably talks less to people and more to God than the average woman. She listens to the voice of the Holy Spirit, Who has been known to whisper, "be quiet" on *many* occasions to *this* wife. In fact, the phrase "keep your mouth shut" is perhaps the most common wisdom the Holy Spirit gives me on a regular basis.

If you struggle with keeping your mouth shut, let me first welcome you to the club. I am the president.

Next, let me refer you to Deborah Smith Pegues' book, *30 Days to Taming Your Tongue*. Every wife would do well by participating in the occasional "tongue fast."

* * * * *

Father, I think You for Your wisdom. Help me yield to Your guidance immediately and fully. Show me who I am in You and help me know what to say and when to be quiet. You promised that the Holy Spirit would guide me into all truth. I receive that promise now in Jesus' name. Amen.

Recommended Reading

My first real job was teaching seventh grade math. It didn't take me long to figure out that I was not a very good seventh grade teacher, so I left the position after only two years. As painful as it was for me to stick through those two years, I left with a strong friendship to a fellow new teacher, Jeanne. She gave me one of my very first books on prayer, and God used her gift to spark a change in my life. Though I was already a believer, I wasn't walking in the fullness of His promises, and I *always* ran from the fellowship of His sufferings (Philippians 3:10). Now, thanks to God's hand on these many authors listed below, my walk grows stronger each day.

Here are ten books that changed my life. I recommend them to you and every woman I know who wants to see God's desires fulfilled in her.

Christenson, Evelyn. *Lord, Change Me*. Wheaton, IL: Victor, 1977.
DeMoss, Nancy Leigh. *Lies Women Believe and the Truth That Sets Them Free*. Chicago: Moody, 2001.

Dobson, James C. *Love Must Be Tough*. Carol Stream, IL: Tynedale House, 2007.

George, Elizabeth. *A Woman after God's Own Heart*. Eugene, Or.: Harvest House, 1997.

Murray, Andrew. *Humility*. Minneapolis, MN: Bethany House, 2001.

Partow, Donna. *Becoming a Vessel God Can Use*. Minneapolis, MN: Bethany House, 2004.

Sherrer, Quin, Ruthanne Garlock, and Beth Feia. *The Making of a Spiritual Warrior: A Woman's Guide to Daily Victory*. Ann Arbor, MI: Vine / Servant Publications, 1998.

Sherrer, Quin and Ruthanne Garlock, *A Woman's Guide to Spiritual Warfare Protect Your Home, Family and Friends from SpiritualDarkness*. Regal, 2010.

Swindoll, Charles R. *Active Spirituality*. [S.l.]: Thomas Nelson Pub, 1994.

Swindoll, Charles R. *Living Above the Level of Mediocrity: A Commitment to Excellence*. Dallas: Word Pub., 1989.

About the Author...

Hey, it's me again. I know, I know—you were expecting a third-person, formal biography starting with the fact that I was born in Ft. Worth, TX. Well, I've never read an author's biography and thought, "Wow! She's from Fort Worth? No wonder I loved this book!" So, here's the real scoop: I'm married with two teenage children, my family lives just outside of Dallas, and I have a Cocker Spaniel who likes to watch televangelists all day.

When I'm not busy procrastinating, I actually do write stuff. So far, I've written seven books (mostly Christian fiction) and I write short, realistic but purposeful fiction for struggling secondary readers (WeGottaRead.com). I used to be a public school teacher, which is where the short stories began. My students gave me lots of dramatic ideas. I left the classroom in 2002 after earning my master's degree and began my career as an educational consultant, which I find tremendously fulfilling.

In addition to writing and training teachers, I encourage women through the Women Growing in Christ blog and through women's ministries at my home church, Oak Cliff Bible Fellowship Church, Pastor Tony Evans. I do some public speaking at conferences and workshops, but not too much. I don't want to miss these last years with my kids at home, plus I'd like to stay married to my first husband. He's pretty cool.

Let's keep in touch via the web!

www.MichelleStimpson.com
www.Facebook.com/Michelle.Stimpson2
www.Twitter.com/MichellStimpson
www.WomenGIC.blogspot.com

In His Love,
Michelle

Made in the USA
Monee, IL
21 November 2020